AF269879

HELP!

My Christian Marriage is Falling Apart

HELP!

My Christian Marriage is Falling Apart

JOSEPH M. BIANCHI

Published by Calvary Press Publishing

© Calvary Press Publishing

ISBN: 978-187-973-7990

All Bible quotes are from the English Standard Version 2001 ESV except where stated otherwise.

All Rights Reserved. No portion of this book may be reproduced without the express written consent of the publisher.

www.calvarypress.com

PRINTED IN USA

Contents

Introduction

Does the world really need another booklet on marriage? Apparently, it does. Marriage is in very bad shape. Although it was once proclaimed that divorce amongst true Bible-believing Christians was equal to, or greater than, non-believers, such is not the case. New statistics show that believers are much less likely to divorce—but it **does** happen.

Indeed, believing Christians are not immune to divorce and marital strife in general. Men and women are sinners. We are born depraved; our wills are in bondage to sin. At times we love our sin much more than we love our spouse. So, if this be the case, what shall we do?

Before we can start to answer questions about what causes marital conflicts and how to resolve them, we must first define what marriage is, and proceed from there. Hence, the title of the first chapter of this book.

Before we go any further, let's talk about what this booklet will be about, and what it will *not be* about.

This booklet will not present you with some kind of formula to instantly make your marriage problems go away. An author could sell millions of books with titles like, *How to Make your Husband Behave!* or *How to Get Your Wife To Do Exactly What You Tell Her!*

However, such books would present you with a fantasy, void of truth or Biblical precepts.

Indeed, this booklet may overlap the information that you may have read in other books. There is no claim here that this booklet reveals truth that has never been heard or seen before. What this booklet will do that you may not have encountered is to get right to the core of what marriage is, and what causes the problems in marriage.

Many books have been written that take a few hundred pages before getting to the real "meat" of the issue, boring and confusing the reader along the way. Hopefully, this short booklet will not do that. Rather, it is designed to give you direct truth from the Word, cutting through any excuses that you or your spouse may have.

If possible, it would be best for both you and your spouse to read this booklet. Yes, there are times when either the husband or the wife is one hundred percent in the wrong—but it is rare.

Usually, conflict arises because both parties have a misunderstanding of what marriage is, and what their duties are within the marriage—it is that simple!

Let us begin.

So, You Think You Know What Marriage Is?

What is marriage?

It seems like such an innocent and easy question. After all, so many people get married, and when they do, certainly they know what marriage is...right?

Go ahead, answer the question for yourself. Think you can?

Sometimes the best way to answer a question is to use the "Oriental Approach." That is, to say what the thing you are describing is ***not***.

In this case, consider the following:

- Marriage is not to satisfy your romantic notions of love—although romance does have something to do with marriage.
- Marriage is not a relationship in which you monitor what you are "getting out of it," viz; your emotional satisfaction.
- Marriage is not a "contract" that when broken, you can get out of.

- Marriage is not just for sexual satisfaction—although sex and bonding go together under God's design.

Ok, did you find any of your definitions in this list? If "yes," then you are going to have to readjust your thinking about marriage, and it may be jarring. If "no," then you will have to allow this book, but most importantly, God's Word, to write upon the black board of your mind something new.

In either case, your preconceived notions will be shattered.

Now, before we can approach the issue of marriage we must first come to the foot of the Creator and study His design for creation in general.

We will not attempt to refute the evolutionary theory of how Man got here. No, we will assume that The Lord God created Man from the dust of the earth, that He created Woman from Adam, and that He has a plan for men and women, for marriage, and for the world.

"In the beginning God created..." These are the opening words of Genesis 1 that are so often misunderstood and maligned. God is a creator God. He creates with a purpose. He is almighty. Yet, consider the foolishness of men and women. Both men and women are sinners and their wills are in bondage to sin. They fool themselves by thinking that they are in control; that they are autonomous and can create their own rules. But men and women are not righteous—they are not even good (Romans 3:10ff)!

Wait! When God created the world, he said that it was "very good" (Genesis 1:31). God created the first man Adam in His own image, a sentient being that could have communion with the Creator.

So what happened? Sin happened.

Adam was set upon this earth, but creation was not yet complete.

In Genesis 2:18, God said that, "It is not good for the man to be alone. I will make a helper suitable for him." Many interpreters will exegete this verse by saying that God realized that Adam was "lonely." This is a very weak and anemic view of this verse.

Again, God is a Creator God with a purpose. Adam had a purpose: to govern the earth and to procreate. Well, he could not do this by himself! Thus, God creates the woman to complete His creation. Adam declares that the woman is, "bone of my bones and flesh of my flesh." In the woman, Eve, Adam sees both his helper who is different from him, and his own reflection. He understands the full impact of Creation, and instantly realizes that he is to be united to his wife.

That is why Scripture then says that men are to "leave their father and mother" and be united to their wives: the two become "one flesh." My friends, can a man cut himself in half and still live? Can a woman pull her heart out, and still be alive? Of course not, and this something that you must grasp if you are having marital difficulties: you must eliminate the prospect of separating from your spouse—it cannot, ever, be an option. This will be discussed in detail later.

So God creates woman and gives both she and Adam a prohibition not to eat of the fruit of the tree in the middle of the garden. But the serpent, Satan disguised, tempts Eve.

What does he tempt her with? Half-truths and lies. He declares that they will not die. Half-truth: they will not die physically, but they will "fall' and die spiritually. Ironically, death will indeed come upon the world because of this sin. Notice that Eve sees the tree as "desirable to make one wise" (Gen. 3:6). This is clearly an over-reach: The Lord God had given a very clear command not to eat of the fruit of the tree, but Eve had a desire to be "wise"; she wanted to discover something, or possess a knowledge that was forbidden to her—a clear act of rebellion.

Herein we see a simple yet plain truth about men and women in general—and about marriages in particular: we tend toward a state of rebellion. Marriages start to fall asunder when we place our foot outside God's prescribed mode of conduct for marital relationships. We are not talking here about some form of "Patriarchy" regarding a woman's relationship to her husband, or a man getting in touch with his "feminine side." We are simply saying that there is a rule of conduct that must be followed within the marital state in order for there to be peace.

Eve partakes of the fruit—and things go downhill from there. She has rebelled, she has sinned.

But wait! If this was the case, why do we call The Fall "Adam's Sin"? Why is Adam then considered the "first sinner"?

Notice what the text says: "...and she gave also to her husband with her, and he ate." Adam was Eve's "covering." He was to take the lead in the marriage by guiding and protecting his wife—especially spiritually. From our text, we see he failed miserably in his task. And this is where many men fail in marriage. They are not providing loving guidance, nor are they protecting their wives. Now, they may *think* they are. "Gee, I kiss her now and then. I provide a nice home. She knows I love the kids—and we even take vacations together!"

Well, all of that is nice, but we are talking about something more involved here. Once again, let's use the approach spoken of at the beginning of this chapter—we will state what manly Biblical headship is *not*:

- It is not being authoritarian and demanding that your wife submit, "or else!"
- It is not providing material goods and luxuries—although there is nothing inherently wrong with these things.
- It is not simply "going places" with your family. If that were the case, they could simply take the dog or the cat!

No, it is none of these things. Rather, it is providing nurturing love, protection and encouragement. It is also being involved in the lives of your family members. Men, you need to be asking your wife and children what is going on in their lives: "How are you doing? Are you OK spiritually and emotionally? Anything new happen this week? You look down—did something happen that upset you?" ...etc...etc.

From the other side, the wife needs to be encouraging and helpful to her husband. Not just in tasks around the house, but by holding him up in prayer, helping him to cope with the pressures of providing for the family and being a true "help meet" for him.

Remember this axiom: Women want to be loved (and respected). Men want to be respected (and loved).

In the following chapters we will, based on what Scripture tells us, flesh out the details of marriage.

Marriage: Covenant Or Contract?

Many trees have been felled to make the paper to write the books on marriage. Certainly, many of these books are accurate in their attempt to help married couples work through their problems. Some are less helpful and devolve into "He said...she said...so now I say [i.e., the author]." We said at the beginning of this booklet that we would get right to the heart of the matter of marital problems—and so we shall.

At the center of most marital problems is the overall concept of how the husband and wife view the married state. Bad behavior in marriage and the attended problems that come with it are simply a manifestation of a misunderstanding of the definition of marriage. Most people, even Christian people, view marriage like a business contract: each side has something they want, and they expect the other side to fulfill that desire. If the contract is not fulfilled to one or the other's satisfaction, it can be broken. After all, the need was not met—or at least not up to husband's or wife's standards or expectations.

Marriage, however, is not a "contractual agreement." No, it is a covenant—a sacred covenant.

What is a covenant?

In the Bible, a covenant is an agreement between God and his people, in which God makes promises to his people and, usually, requires certain conduct from them. In the Old Testament, God made agreements with Noah, Abraham, and Moses.

One of the many things that Christians seem to skim over when studying their Bible is the solemnity of these covenants. They form parts of the essential pillars of God's plan of salvation, ultimately fulfilled in the vicarious death of Christ. They are not just "nice stories" remembered from childhood Sunday School. Rather, they show the seriousness of God's dealing with men and woman.

In Genesis 6, the Lord God sees the increasing wickedness of humankind, and that the thoughts of men and women were "evil continually" (Gen. 6:5). Therefore, God sent the universal flood to destroy all that is living. But Scripture tells us, "Noah found favor in the eyes of the Lord." It was God's plan to preserve humankind through Noah and his offspring. After the flood waters subsided, Noah built an altar to the Lord God and made offerings that pleased the Lord. In His sovereignty, the Lord promised never to destroy the earth again by a flood. As a mark of this covenant, He set a "bow in the cloud" that when God Himself looks upon it, He would remember His covenant with humankind and never destroy the Earth with a flood again.

What many average Christians, and Bible scholars for that matter, overlook, is that the bow (i.e., the "rainbow") is also a symbol of war. Picture a warrior, if you will, with his "*bow* and arrow." Note that when a rainbow appears, the bow is facing upward. Now picture an arrow in that bow facing up at the heavens.

Consider this: What the Lord God is saying is that if He breaks this covenant, He would, if it were possible, destroy Himself!

Does this seem like a general "business contract" to you? Have you ever hired a contractor that said he would literally kill himself if the job was not completed or done improperly? Many a homeowner could only wish for this!

Consider what God did when Abraham opined that he did not have any heirs. He did not say to Abraham, "Well, Ok, here's the deal: I will make every effort to give you offspring, if it does not work out, our contract will be void!"

No, rather he "cut" a covenant—literally. He commanded Abraham to bring Him a heifer, a female goat, a ram, a turtledove and a young pigeon (Gen. 15:9ff). With the exception of the birds, the animals were then cut in half and placed opposite each other. When the sun went down, Scripture states that, "a deep sleep fell upon Abram; and behold, terror *and* great darkness fell upon him." Now, many of us have been in a lawyer's office for a variety of reasons and we have had some dread, but we can be assured it was nothing like Abraham's. The God of the universe was making a covenant with him—and it was not casual or breakable. The Lord promised Abraham both descendants and land. Neither God nor Abraham could "cancel" this covenant; God could never rescind the promise, and Abraham could not deny that which was promised to him!

Since marriage is a "Creation ordinance," created by God in the beginning, it is not something that is breakable; it is a "forever covenant." While there is much emotion tied to marriage, the concept of marriage itself is not an emotional thing. Rather, it is quite rational. The God of the Bible is a purposeful, rational and creative being who is sovereign over all things. He is also, "not the author of confusion" (1 Cor. 14:33).

In 2 Samuel 7, Nathan the prophet is commanded by God to speak to David and tell him that God will make him, "...a great name, like the names of the great men who are on the earth" (2 Sam 7:9). The Lord also promised to "make a house" for David, not a literal one, but rather descendants that will follow after him—a "dynasty," if you will. In the Biblical story of redemption, this promise is most important because the sense of the text is that Messiah will come from the progeny of David as God will, "establish the throne of his kingdom forever" (2 Sam. 7:13).

God made a promise to David. Could He break it? Could He "take it back" and declare it null and void? Certainly not. It was a pivotal promise (i.e., covenant) that was to be fulfilled.

Marriage also is a covenant created by God and *cannot* be broken. You must take the worldly idea that marriage is simply "an agreement" that you can "get out of" when things don't suit you, or when your spouse doesn't behave the way *you* want them to.

When two sinners come together under one roof there is bound to be problems, but there is no escape hatch to permanently end the relationship. Marriage is a sacred covenant. You must expunge the concept of "separation" or "divorce" from your list of possibilities. Then, and only then, can you begin to face marital problems that exist now—or in the future.

Yes, There Is A Difference!

In the age we are living in, the idea that men and women are different has become anathema. The media and its liberal pundits have effectively neutralized all differences in the sexes. But God's purposes in creation do not change. God has created two distinct sexes: male and female—and, yes, they are very different. They are different physiologically, emotionally and spiritually. Men and women were designed with a purpose; both are made in the image of God, but with different assignments. They are to complement one another in order to do the work of giving glory to God. Both are human, but they have different emotional needs, perceive things differently—and were uniquely designed for different tasks.

Of course, to many people the aforementioned description constitutes "fighting words" as they go against the grain of modern culture.

And this is the heart of where a lot of modern married couples go off course. Simply put, they are trying to live their lives and solve conflicts based on the benchmark of the world, and not the Bible.

They may even *think* that they are following biblical guidelines, when, in fact, they are acting as worldly as their unsaved neighbor.

But they are not necessarily to blame.

Not only has the media confused the issue of marriage and the nature of men and women, but, sad to say, the contemporary church has, too.

What many couples hear from the pulpit is simply stylized psychology with a veneer of Christian principles. A watered down gospel or, worse yet, outright heresy, can never produce good results in any realm. This is certainly true when it comes to marriage and the roles of men and women.

Many denominations have walked back their previous convictions on the roles of men and women, as well as "gender identity." What constitutes female virtues or "manliness" has been repackaged into something it was never meant to be. Indeed, this is not just some sort of minor shift to contextualize the gospel, this is rather a re-definition of what it means to be male and female—and it has played itself out by many churches accepting same-sex marriage.

We have often heard the canard that Jesus, in the course of His ministry, never spoke about sexuality; that He never clearly defined the roles of men and women. This is so false as to be mind bending. When the Pharisees bring up the issue of divorce in Matthew 19, Jesus begins his reply with, ""Have you not read that He who created *them* from the beginning MADE THEM MALE AND FEMALE..." (v.4) Thus, Jesus, God incarnate, proclaims that there are indeed, two sexes, and that these two opposite sexes are the only choice when it comes to marriage. There is no nuance in the above quote: there is male, and there is female—and they are to be joined in a "one flesh" relationship that is unbreakable: "What therefore God has joined together, let no man separate" (v.6).

There is no getting around the fact that men and women have different make-ups emotionally and spiritually speaking. Without these distinctions the created order God intended unravels. Gender distinctions were created to complement each other; to give glory to God by their very differences.

Often times, these differences are contained in how we "hear" things. A husband saying, he is going to the office or fishing on his day off, may be "heard" by the wife as, "You are not as important to me as my pursuits." A wife innocently commenting on the success of her friend's husband may be heard by her own husband as, "Why can't you be as successful?"

These things are not abnormal; they arise from the natural thinking patterns of two people under the influence of the Fall. That is not to say that interactions between husband and wife cannot be improved, but rather there are natural patterns to our emotional natures that differ between the sexes.

In matters of life husband and wife must walk in agreement. That, however, does not mean that there isn't a substantial amount of give and take before a decision is made. Moreover, the two sides may have different approaches as to how a decision is made. Women tend to do a lot more verbalizing to "lay things out" so that the situation hand can be understood. Men tend to internalize their thoughts, and this can be interpreted by the woman as not being "engaged."

Above and beyond these things is the covenant relationship. Every period of a marriage is governed by the knowledge that it is a God ordained relationship. There may be misunderstandings, even deep wounds, but these are over shadowed by the knowledge that the Lord God has put you into this relationship, with all your differences. Those differences may, at times, make you want to exclaim, "What am I doing with this person?" Again, the answer is simple: God put you together with your mate.

"Could it be," you may ask, "that there has been some terrible mistake?"

No. The Creator has placed you with precisely the right person, although with our human eyes that may be hard to see!

If that be the case, then any problem that arises must be worked out with the notion that there was no mistake made, that there are no exit doors—and that a solution must be found other than a split.

There are marriages whose problems may be extremely severe. The question that must be asked, initially, in these circumstances, is not, "Who is in the wrong?"—but, rather, has the main conflict arisen out of one spouse's sin, or simply because there are differences in perception that need to be understood. Many times, husbands and wives will have a "blow up" that results in an epiphany: Both sides go at it and may reveal things that the other has never heard before—and the result may be, "Wow, I didn't know you felt that way about thus and so..." And a new understanding is born.

Of course, the main topic of many books on marriage is communication. It is an essential element to keeping peace between you and your spouse—and it is something that needs to be cultivated on a day-to-day basis. We will not be spending a lot of time on this topic; it has been covered in full in many titles. However, it is axiomatic that if some decision needs to be made, either of a life changing nature or a mundane one, open and honest communication needs to be the rule of the day. More importantly, in all situations, it is *how* we communicate that is the bellwether of our spouse's response. We may have a good grasp of the situation, but we may convey it in a way that seems threatening or disrespectful to the other. The result may be that the subject becomes a "hot potato" that neither of you want to discuss. Thus, the problem never gets solved.

One of the essential ingredients of a covenantal relationship is *patience*. For many believing Christians, the fact that the Lord was patient in His dealing with them prior to conversion is enough to shut down all complaints during stressful times. As Israel wandered in the wilderness, the rebelliousness of the people was so severe that we are amazed at the incredible grace shown to them by God. These "stiff necked" people tried the patience of the Lord time after time. Yet, God's covenant stood, and the ultimate result was the manifestation of Jesus Christ in the flesh, fully God, fully human, making atonement for His people (Matt. 1:21), the elect of God.

So it is to be expected that that you and your spouse, by the very nature of your make-up as man and woman, will have differences. A marriage that never has conflicts is a marriage where the philosophy is, "I really don't care!"

Differences naturally mean opposing views. You might have entered the marriage covenant thinking that conflict is to be eschewed. However, good things can be hatched from conflict. In western society, much energy is spent avoiding conflict, and trying to ensure that things move along smoothly without any bumps in the road. The abuse of drugs and alcohol is a testimony to the excesses that men and women will go through to numb the negative side of life. But there is just no getting around the fact that our world is fallen, and we are going to have to face trials and tribulations, some of which will be incredibly severe.

Conflicts in marriage can push the relationship to the breaking point. So how do we make our marriages "unbreakable"?

The answer lies in the Cross.

Is The Cross
In Your Marriage?

There is an old saying of movie and song that has become that great cliché declared by couples around the globe: "You and me against the world!"

Certainly, many couples will meet opposition from outside their own relationships. Hopefully, this will not be because they are doing something wrong or behaving in a way that is ungodly. Sometimes they are meeting opposition because they *are* doing the right thing. But the real question is: Is marriage a private affair only between the husband and the wife?

The answer to that question is a resounding, "NO!"

First, since marriage is a covenant, others attest to it. Most marriage ceremonies are public affairs; there are invited guests who witness the couple taking their vows who promise to "love, honor and obey." Even if the couple has a closed wedding where only the celebrant, the minister or judge, hears them taking their vows—there are witnesses. How a couple behaves in public, and how they treat each other in private, is the business of society in general. Why? Again, because marriage is at the root of the societal mores that God has created.

Certainly, in our era this sounds strange indeed. Isn't marriage a very private situation? No, it is not.

The notion that marriage is a private affair is a worldly one. God has created marriage as an ensign to the nations; the building block of creation and all the morals that go with it. It is also symbolic of the church.

> This mystery is profound, and I am saying that it refers to Christ and the church
>
> —Eph. 5:32

In Ephesians 5, the apostle Paul is describing how believers should walk in love. The second half of the chapter is dedicated to husbands and wives, and is very instructive and insightful. The aforementioned verse is his conclusion. We mention it in reverse order because it is so important, so pivotal, that we need to have this fixed in our minds if we expect to understand the meaning of marriage. Marriage is not a vestige of our "evolutionary past," or a creation of man's concept of union. It is amazing that so many secularists and atheists get married when they do not have the faintest idea of what it is, and what is expected of them.

Paul clearly states that marriage "refers to Christ and the church." Therefore, a non-believer cannot truly apprehend the obligations of marriage. Yet, before God, their marriage is valid—and they are held to the same marriage standards as believers because those marriage standards are a supernatural decree, whether they choose to recognize it or not.

So, in the passage in question, what is Paul's instruction for women?

> [22] Wives, submit to your own husbands, as to the Lord. [23] For the husband is the head of the wife even as Christ is the head of the church, his body, and is himself its Savior. [24] Now as

the church submits to Christ, so also wives should submit in everything to their husbands.

In today's culture, these words can start a riot. Women submitting? Isn't that the basis for all abuse of women in our culture? Wasn't the patriarchal nature of the church forced on society over the past two millennia—and is this not the reason for the suppression of women across all cultures?

Quite the opposite is true. In the ancient world women were little more than chattel, to be done with however the husband pleased. Christianity brought honor to women and elevated their status. Instead of being thought of as property, they were now spiritually equal to men as, of course, they had always been in the eyes of God. Keep in mind also, it was women that Christ revealed his resurrection to first (Matt. 28:1-10). Women accompanied both Christ and Paul in their ministries.

In the times that the New Testament was written, this was nothing short of revolutionary. We would note that while men and women are equal in God's eyes, their roles are certainly different, as we have discussed earlier, and as will discussed further in this book. Nevertheless, we will state categorically that it was Christianity that liberated women. However, whether we are male or female, liberation is not total freedom to do as we please. In fact, for both sexes, liberation is *dependency* and *submission* to Jesus Christ.

As a Christian, your behavior and manner of life, including your marriage, is bound together in Christ. Your marriage is not a separate entity from your daily life. Since one of the goals of marriage is holiness, it is essential that the cross is at the center of your marriage.

But what does this mean?

Many view the cross in romantic fashion. The cross, to some, is a symbol of love. Indeed, it certainly is that, but it is much more. The cross represents, in fact, the vicarious death of Christ to save "His people" from their sins (Matt. 1:21). It also represents submission: as Christ submitted to the Father's will, so must we submit to the will of Christ. The meaning of Christianity is never "getting something." Quite the opposite, it means giving something, namely, yourself in the cause of Christ.

The apostle Paul reminds us that our whole course of thinking should be to think of others first: Do *nothing from selfishness or empty conceit, but with humility of mind regard one another as more important than yourselves...* Phil. 2:3

Meditate on this verse; like it sink deeply into your mind and soul. It is possible that this one verse will hold the key to **saving your marriage**, or *making your marriage **stronger***.

When we think of the welfare of our spouse before our needs and wants are met, we create an atmosphere of love. Christ put the needs of His people before His own. That need was for salvation. Even as He prayed, knowing the cross was in His near future, He submitted: Going a little farther, He fell with His face to the ground and prayed, *"My Father, if it is possible, may this cup be taken from me. Yet not as I will, but as you will."* Matt. 26:39

"Yet not as I will, but as you will."

This is the call to both the church and the individual Christian. The Church's duty—and your duty—is to serve others. Unfortunately, the church today is filled with people that are simply there to hear a sermon and socialize. They may even agree with the truths in Scripture—but they are being disobedient: their first intentions are not to serve others, but to "get something" from the church or their fellow Christians. Additionally, they want to worship in a way that is pleasing to them, rather than to the God of Creation. In a word, they are "self-absorbed."

There is simply no way that, this attitude being the case, it will not carry itself into a marriage. You may be the culprit, or you may be married to one. Either way, if this is the case, the problem must be dealt with.

> For we who live are constantly being delivered over to death
> for Jesus' sake, so that the life of Jesus also may be manifested
> in our mortal flesh.   —2 Cor. 4:11

In order to live, you have to "die"—die to self, selfish ambitions, and actions that purposely, or even innocently, hurt others. In marriage, we are constantly faced with situations wherein we have to decide whether to die to self and serve our spouse, or continue in our selfish ambitions and behavior. Your marriage, therefore, is a microcosm of the church and the Christian life. How you behave in your marriage will certainly be a barometer of what your opinion is of the Christian life—for good or bad.

Have you "died" in your marriage? This means not only abandoning your selfish ideas and attitudes; it means dealing with someone—your spouse—who may *not* have. And how will you react? With anger or frustration—or even thoughts of divorce? The reality is you will be put into situations that are most difficult for you to handle, no matter how sanguine your spouse may be. Again, when two people are put into close quarters, there is bound to be conflict. This certainly does not mean that your marriage was a mistake. It simply means that you are human.

Your life as a married person is radically different than when you were single. As a single person you could satisfy your whims at a moment's notice. You could go where and when you wanted to, spend your money as you would like—and even emotionally get out of control with people you were not living with and not have to deal with them at the end of the day.

Now, all these things must be filtered through your relationship with your spouse. You must consider what makes your husband or wife happy first. You must think about whether your actions will help or harm your spouse. Most importantly, you will have to discern the long-term implications of whatever decisions you make. While this is certainly true of the wife, it is especially true of the husband if he is operating in his proper role. He is the loving "head" of the relationship, submitting himself to the better welfare of his wife.

Note that everything Christ said or did was for the benefit of others. His very incarnation speaks to the selfless compassion that He had for sinful humanity:

> ...who being in the form of God, did not regard equality with God a thing to be grasped, but emptied Himself, taking the form of a bondservant, and being made in the likeness of men. —Phil. 2:6-7

Christ, being God incarnate, did not have to grasp at divinity; he was divine. Therefore, if Christ, the creator of all things (Col. 1:16) can lower himself to us, certainly, you can consider what's best for your spouse and put aside your selfish desires. Humanity would be totally without hope if Christ did not incarnate, die a vicarious death on the cross, and resurrect. If He did that for sinners who are in constant rebellion against the Creator, you can sacrifice for your spouse.

Note that Christ's sacrifice cuts through all our excuses. Knowing that the Cross lay ahead of Him, He did not turn back:

> He went away again a second time and prayed, saying, "My Father, if this cannot pass away unless I drink it, Your will be done." —Matt. 26:42

Is the will of God being done in your marriage? Are you submitting to each other just as Christ submitted His will to the Father?

If not, you must ask yourself what is the sticking point; you must reflect on your own relationship with Christ. Indeed, you must be sure that you are "in the faith" and applying your faith to your marriage in everything that you do.

The *real* issue in problem marriages is not two individuals at loggerheads with each other, but the individual at loggerheads *with God*.

As we shall see, it the way your covenantal relationship with God goes, so shall your marriage go.

We will discuss this in the next chapter.

5

Your God-Ward Relationship And Your Marriage

To talk about two people in a married relationship is to talk about each one's relationship with God.

In a Christian marriage, the measure of a sound relationship is whether each individual is walking rightly before Christ, or whether there is some underlying sin or rebellion.

It stands to reason that if one of the marriage partners is out of fellowship with God, the marriage will suffer; everything will be out of kilter. Of course, it is possible, and is the case many times, that both spouses are in rebellion against God, and need to have this situation remedied.

Sin is an assault on God. We often think of sin as *man-ward*: we may have done something to hurt another individual; have acted badly—cheated, stolen, lied or physically assaulted them.

But *all sin* is against God.

Let us recall David's sin with Bathsheba (2 Sam. 11). The trouble started by a shirking of responsibility. David decided to stay home in Jerusalem while he sent his army out to fight. This could be termed a form of rebellion against his kingly responsibilities. With time on his hands, he is walking on the palace roof admiring the view when he sees a beautiful woman taking a bath on her roof—and he desires her. The problem is that this woman is married. He quickly ignores this fact, sends for her, and they commit fornication—and she conceives.

A sense of dread seizes him as he fears this act of adultery will be found out. What to do? His idea is to place Uriah, Bathsheba's husband, in the front lines of the battle, and then have the troops around him withdrawn, an assured death sentence. And so, it was. In the text, we see that Uriah was an honorable and faithful man to the King and to God, making the crime much more horrendous.

When David's sin is revealed, he repents with some of the most memorable words from scripture,

> Against You, You only, I have sinned
> And done what is evil in Your sight,
> So that You are justified when You speak
> And blameless when You judge.   —Psalm 51:4

David had seduced a married woman, then had her husband killed to cover up the crime. Yet, in this verse, there is only one that has been sinned against: God and God only.

In the age we are living in, even Christians do not fully comprehend the absolute holiness of God. Anything that violates His absolute holiness is sin. Often, we have a very casual attitude toward our behavior: "That's just the way I am," "I may have done such-and such, but I was right in doing it," "You made me angry, that is why I ...." Such excuses fall to the ground when they happen before the Creator of all things.

There is an obvious and direct correlation between this and your marriage.

When you act poorly toward your spouse, you are actually sinning against God. It is not an act of selfishness toward your spouse, although in a sense it is; it is really open rebellion against God. Additionally, we may even say it is an offense to His church. Marriage, as we have pointed out, is a picture of Christ and His church. Thus, when you act poorly toward your spouse, you are mocking the church!

Perhaps you have never thought of it that way. If not, you need to implant this thought deeply in your mind and let it act as a directive to your behavior.

Before you are tempted to react to something your spouse has said or done, you must first see your response as a direct dialog with God. This may sound rather odd at first, but it is perfectly natural when we understand God's intended relationship with us and Himself.

You were purchased with a purpose. As a believer you must understand that God's election plan places you in an enviable position as opposed to your past.

> [13] In Him, you also, after listening to the message of truth, the gospel of your salvation—having also believed, you were sealed in Him with the Holy Spirit of promise, [14] who is given as a pledge of our inheritance, with a view to the redemption of God's own possession, to the praise of His glory.
>
> —Eph. 1:13-14

If your spouse is a believer, then your relationship is to "the praise of His glory." If your spouse is not a believer, you must still exhibit this glory through your kindness and consideration of his or her wellbeing, while you diligently pray for your husband's or wife's conversion.

An added benefit of all this should be an elevated sense of what God expects in our daily walk. As we walk closer to Him in obedience, we will walk closer to our spouse. Obviously, the converse is true—if we distance ourselves from our relationship with God, our relationship with our spouse will deteriorate.

Somewhere in our self-absorbed society we got the idea that we can separate marriage from our spiritual life. This, of course, is impossible as marriage is integral to our spiritual life. Again, just as Christ cannot separate Himself from the church that He purchased with His blood, so too a man and woman cannot separate themselves from each other once they are under the covenant of marriage.

When a marriage starts to go downhill, many times it can be traced to spiritual declension. Husbands and wives are either not putting enough effort into studying God's word, or they are flatly disobeying. Spiritual hypocrisy is a very common malady; it affects all of us at one time or another. But left to itself, it is a marriage killer!

You can read many books on the things that cause trouble in a marriage without really getting to the heart of the matter. What we are saying here is that you cannot drive around your relationship with Christ, and expect that you will have peace in your marriage.

That is not to say that there are many things that spark conflict. But the solution will always be the same: your vertical relationship—you and Christ.

With this in mind, we will now turn to the issue of conflicts.

6

Conflict: Natural or Unnatural?

In the 21st century we have gotten the false notion that leading the "good life" means the absence of conflict. We feel that we deserve the best of everything: the best school, the best spouse, the best health—and the best bank account.

When something comes along to jar us out of this pipe dream, we are ruffled. "How dare something bad happen to me! I deserve better!"

Our spiritual forefathers knew better. During and after the Protestant Reformation many were burned at the stake for what they believed—and they went gladly to their deaths knowing that they were standing up for what was biblical and just. They knew that their "light affliction" as the apostle Paul calls it (2 Cor. 4:17) was working a greater spiritual good.

Do you feel the same way about your marriage? Is it working a greater good? Moreover, it probably should not feel like a "light affliction" at all, but a blessing.

For many, the idea that their marriage is a blessing is marred by the reality that they are living, if not in open conflict, in an uneasy truce.

We have already pointed out that when you mix male and female, different backgrounds and different personalities, that there is bound to be conflict. A famous comedian once said, "My wife and I were happy for 20 years—and then we met!"

Is that how you look at your marriage? Do you long for the days when you were single? Certainly, you might very well. But you are putting a romantic veneer on those memories of yours. Really, were your single years conflict free? You may have had job troubles, or family troubles; you may have longed for a spouse because you were so terribly lonely! Remember?

If you were not into "biblical courting," then you may have had many failed relationships, had your heart broken many times—and said and did things that you now regret.

OK, the point has been made. Life was not ideal when you were single, because that is how life is—fraught with heartaches and trouble. That certainly doesn't mean that there isn't joy. You can have joy, and you can have it in your marriage, even if there is conflict—because these things flow naturally out of life, so you really should stop kicking against it.

Even Christians behave like "pleasure sharks" at times: constantly swimming looking for something pleasurable to feast on, and when they come across their prey, they park there thinking that this particular pleasure will never end, forgetting that "pleasure" is not the primary thing you were designed for.

You must face the reality that husbands and wives disagree—ok, argue—at times and that this state of affairs is *perfectly natural*. Get used to it.

How do we know when this state of affairs becomes *unnatural*? Answer: when it becomes the *constant* state of affairs.

If a husband and wife are constantly arguing, fussing and generally miserable, then they are in a situation that needs correcting. Something is out of kilter in the spiritual realm. Usually, it's rebellion.

As has been mentioned earlier, men and women are rebellious creatures—yes, even Christian men and women. Really, if the apostle Paul wrestled with besetting and remaining sin, it follows that we would too:

> 21 I find then the principle that evil is present in me, the one who wants to do good. 22 For I joyfully concur with the law of God in the inner man, 23 but I see a different law in the members of my body, waging war against the law of my mind and making me a prisoner of the law of sin which is in my members. 24 Wretched man that I am! Who will set me free from the body of this death? 25 Thanks be to God through Jesus Christ our Lord! So then, on the one hand I myself with my mind am serving the law of God, but on the other, with my flesh the law of sin. —Romans 7:21-25

The formula is a dangerous one: two sinners with remaining sin joined together for the rest of their natural lives. They must eat, drink, work out their schedules, decide how to use their money, when and where to vacation—and how to raise the children, together.

They each carry idiosyncratic behavior that the other has to deal with. They will correct each other, because, after all, each one *knows* that the other is wrong. They will go through illnesses, job loss, ageing and retirement together.

Finally, one will die, and the other will have to deal with the loss.

In all these things there will be conflict. Have no doubt.

The key to defusing conflict is to regard your spouse as "better than yourself" (Phil. 2:3). Again, this does not mean you cannot, even with vigor, debate an issue. It does mean that you must consider the needs of your spouse *first*. What does he/she need in this situation? If my husband/wife is that committed to their position, it must mean a lot to them—how can I meet their need?

This is the essence of "a covenant relationship"; it does not exist to meet one person's needs, but, rather, for the mutual benefit of both.

Clearly, your effort to satisfy your spouse will, in the log run, have positive benefits for you. First, you will spiritually be right before God. That enables you to have peace. Constantly battling for your objective will produce a chronic anger that will destroy you and your spouse. Second, when your spouse sees that you are willing to meet his/her needs, they most likely will reciprocate and, therefore, there will be times when he or she will acquiesce to your desires. It is a win/win situation.

You may quickly rejoin, "But what if my mate is totally intransigent. What if they have no intention of changing? Then what?"

Well, first, you remain true to the Covenant. You continue to pray and honor your spouse despite his/her refusal to repent or change.

Moreover, you continue to believe what God says about Himself and His ability to change your spouse.

There are no doubt times we would like to throw up our hands and just walk away from a situation. But scripture is clear that we cannot. We must continually move forward in faith. Indeed, this may entail suffering, something 21st century men and women go out of their way to avoid.

Despite conflict, your marriage should be held together by, we'll say it again, the covenant you made with each other before God.

You may reply, "Easier said then done! My spouse is impossible to live with—and is even threatening."

OK, no one can brush away the intense difficulties of marriage, especially when the threat of violence raises its head. Does violence in a marriage constitute the breaking of the covenant? It certainly does, just like infidelity would.

But here is the question: Does anything **permanently** destroy the "one flesh" relationship of marriage?

7

A Forever Broken Covenant?

At what point can we say that the "one flesh" covenant has been permanently broken?

When this question is asked, we immediately think of adultery. The general evangelical line of thinking has adopted a very casual view of divorce and remarriage. The idea here is that adultery breaks the "one flesh covenant." Indeed, it does—it is a gross violation of God's view of marriage fidelity.

The question we want to deal with, however, is: can the marriage covenant be *permanently* broken?

In business, when the agreements in a contract are broken, one party may sue the other to get satisfaction.

In the case of a contemporary marriage, it is not only common to sue for divorce when there is overt adultery; but many marriages end for all kinds of reasons.

In 1969, California became the first state to institute "no fault divorce." The purpose of this was to make divorce possible for a number of reasons, without impugning any one party.

Thus, this law allowed for divorce for disagreements on how to raise the children, disagreements over finances, the couples work arrangements, and even "lack of communication."

Consider that in Jesus' time, a man could divorce his wife also for a number of reasons—even for burning his dinner!

Now, did Jesus hold to this same standard? Many evangelical Christians today would say no; Jesus only permits divorce when there is adultery. And yet, there is not a complete consensus on this matter.

The two New Testament verses that are in view are Matt. 19:3–12 and Matt. 5:32.

They read as follows:

3 And Pharisees came up to him and tested him by asking, "Is it lawful to divorce one's wife for any cause?" 4 He answered, "Have you not read that he who created them from the beginning made them male and female, 5 and said, 'Therefore a man shall leave his father and his mother and hold fast to his wife, and the two shall become one flesh'? 6 So they are no longer two but one flesh. What therefore God has joined together, let not man separate." 7 They said to him, "Why then did Moses command one to give a certificate of divorce and to send her away?" 8 He said to them, "Because of your hardness of heart Moses allowed you to divorce your wives, but from the beginning it was not so. 9 And I say to you: whoever divorces his wife, except for sexual immorality, and marries another, commits adultery."

10 The disciples said to him, "If such is the case of a man with his wife, it is better not to marry." 11 But he said to them, "Not everyone can receive this saying, but only those to whom it is given. 12 For there are eunuchs who have been so from birth, and there are eunuchs who have been made eunuchs by men, and there are eunuchs who have made themselves eunuchs for

the sake of the kingdom of heaven. Let the one who is able to receive this receive it."

³² But I say to you that everyone who divorces his wife, except on the ground of sexual immorality, makes her commit adultery, and whoever marries a divorced woman commits adultery.

Notice that in the first reference, the Pharisees ask Jesus if it is lawful to divorce for "any cause." They were obviously testing him to see if he was in agreement with both the teaching of Moses, and the teaching of the Rabbis.

Note that Jesus refers them right back to Genesis. He does not debate them, nor does he give a nuance on the accepted teaching. His statement is quite plain, "What God has joined together, let not man separate." He tells them Moses permitted it because of the "hardness of their heart." The exception? Adultery. The second reference in Matt. 5 says the same thing. This is what is known as the "exception clause."

Now, you might think that these verses put the whole issue to rest. But wait. Mark 10 records either the same incident as Matt. 19, or another time where he is tested again. In this case, there is no exception. Jesus states again that man is not to separate what God has joined together. In Mark 10:10, the disciples ask him again about the matter. Why did they do this? Most likely because they could not come to grips with what Jesus was saying! "Jesus, do you really mean that a man can never divorce his wife?" may be a good guess as to what they were thinking.

His answer?:

"Whoever divorces his wife and marries another commits adultery against her, ¹² and if she divorces her husband and marries another, she commits adultery."

There is no "exception" here. Jesus' answer is unequivocal:

there is to be no divorce.

There have been commentators who claim that the so-called "exception clause" refers to the "espousal" or "betrothal period." The betrothal period in Jesus' day was much like an engagement—but more so. Basically, you were married, but the marriage was not consummated yet. The man and woman did not live together at this time, but still referred to each other as "husband" and "wife." Sexual relations did not take place until the marriage ceremony where the marriage was formalized. They would then retire to a bed chamber to consummate the marriage—and the wedding celebration would then continue.

Recall that when Mary conceived Jesus by the Holy Spirit before Joseph was aware of what was going on, he intended on "putting her away" in a private manner. This is divorce for the sin of immorality—and this is what many commentators believe Jesus was referring to in his "exception." The divorce would have been legitimate because they had not had sexual relations together, and one of the parties was unfaithful.

There are other commentators who believe that Jesus was referring to some form of "uncleanness," but not necessarily adultery. It could be that the couple realizes that they are somehow close relations, like cousins, and didn't know it.

We must also include here Luke 16:18, where there is also no exception:

> [18] "Everyone who divorces his wife and marries another commits adultery, and he who marries a woman divorced from her husband commits adultery."

Do you see how serious our Lord takes marriage and the issue of divorce? God hates divorce and He expects a married couple to stay that way. We live in an age of easy divorce and remarriage. But the marriage covenant is never really nullified by man. It is God's intention that you stay with your spouse "until death do you part."

If you are having serious trouble in your marriage, before you even see a biblical counselor, *eliminate the idea of divorce completely first.*

What if you are experiencing severe emotional or physical abuse?

In the case of abuse, the wife or the husband has every right to protect themselves, and may use legal means to do so. It is not, axiomatic, however, that such action should always lead to divorce. Prayer is a powerful weapon when confronting marital difficulties.

There may be instances where the husband and wife need to physically separate for a time, but two-way communication always needs to be present.

This is obviously a difficult issue. But nothing is impossible for God—His desire is to heal your marriage.

Some Healing Guidelines

We have attempted in this booklet to express how important it is to understand the marriage covenant. The God of the Bible means what he says in his laws and covenants. We thus must obey.

We should not, however, feel that obedience is a life-sentence to misery. The Christian life is not easy, although many false teachers today would like us to think so. Marriage is not easy, although there are many "How To" books about marriage on the market that claim they have a system to cure your marriage woes.

No human author can give you any guarantees about your marriage relationship. We can guarantee that the Scriptures declare that husband and wife are to stay together throughout their lives; that whatever roadblocks appear during this time must be dealt with in a biblical manner—and that there is to be no divorce.

So, let us briefly summarize what you have just read, and how this can be helpful to you:

- Marriage is a covenant created by God.
- The marriage bond can never be broken as the "two become

one" when the vows are made.

- No judge or magistrate can therefore break the marriage covenant
- Conflict in marriage is normal and may even lead to a closer relationship.
- Disagreements in marriage, even vigorous conflict, must be solved through biblical precepts.
- The Lord wants you to mature and grow closer to Him as you grow closer to each other.

Life in the 21st century can be extremely complicated, leading to greater stress on marriages. But we have the Bible to guide us—an infallible book of absolute truth.

Let us keep that in mind and give glory to God as we walk through a fallen world as husband and wife.

Printed in the United States
by Baker & Taylor Publisher Services